REMOVE CHILD BEFORE FOLD

The *101 Stupidest,* *Silliest,* and *Wackiest* *Warning Labels Ever*

By Bob Dorigo Jones

WARNING!
Reading this book will be ideal for lifting your spirits and not taking life too seriously.

WARNER BOOKS
New York   Boston

363.
19
J
c. 1

Warner Books
Hachette Book Group USA
1271 Avenue of the Americas
New York, NY 10020
Visit our Web site at www.HachetteBookGroupUSA.com.

Printed in the United States of America

First Edition: January 2007
10 9 8 7 6 5 4 3 2 1

Library of Congress Control Number: 2006923302
ISBN-13: 978-0-446-69656-2
ISBN-10: 0-446-69656-0

Book design and interior illustrations by Mada Design, Inc.
Cover design by Brigid Pearson
Cover illustration by A. J. Garces

DEDICATED TO...

Bobby and Johnny Dorigo Jones and
my partner in all things,
Denise Dorigo Jones

Also, special thanks to Mike Dalere
and editor Jason Pinter

ACKNOWLEDGMENTS

*T*he author hereby thanks the following parties, heretofore referred to as friends, for their assistance, support, and encouragement:

Steven B. Hantler, John M. Engler, Philip K. Howard, Walter Olson, Samina Schey, John Thomas, and Richard Thornburgh.

Dan Abrams, Mitch Albom, Tom Brokaw, Dawson Bell, Catherine Crier, Lou Dobbs, Paul Harvey, José Martinez, Dennis Miller, Keith Olbermann, Rush Limbaugh, Dick Purtan, and John Stossel.

James Barrett, Randy Cassingham, Neil Coughlan, Brian Fabiano, Marty Habalewsky, Paul Hillegonds, Kevin Kelly, William Kemp, Robert LaBrant, William Lucas, Al Mann, John MacIlroy, Joe Petito, Betsy Pickering, Marsha Rabiteau, Victor Schwartz, Bob Skowronek, Congressman Lamar Smith, Duane Tarnacki, Lucille Taylor, Bill Weber, Kendall Wingrove, and James Percelay, author of *Whiplash! America's Most Frivolous Lawsuits*.

Michigan Lawsuit Abuse Watch, M-LAW, board members (past and present): Beth Thieme; Angelo S. Lanni; Dr. William B. Allen; Betty Jean Awrey; Tommy Brann; Agostinho Fernandes; David A. Herz, MD; Albert J. Koegel; William Laimbeer Jr.; Edward A. Loniewski, DO; Dr. Lawrence W. Reed; Michael Sandler, MD; Mary Ellen Sheets; Bill Shepler; Reid Thebault; and Ted Wahby.

The American Justice Partnership: Dan Pero, Steve Nowlan, and Kristyn Shayon.

The American Tort Reform Association: Sherman "Tiger" Joyce.

Common Good: Franklin Stone and Paul Barringer.

The staff at HQ Global in Novi, Michigan: Sara Baer and Kristen Quinn.

And Robert B. Jones Sr., Tamara S. Jones, Alice L. Dorigo, and Gabriella M. Serentha.

INTRODUCTION

*H*ave you seen any good warning labels lately? Of course you have. They're almost everywhere you look.

From the moment in the morning when you raise your head off a pillow bearing that famous Do Not Remove warning tag, to the second you drop back in bed at night, you are bombarded with warnings. And a special form of warning label, the wacky warning label, can now be found on all kinds of consumer products.

There are sleeping pills that warn, "May cause drowsiness" and fishing lures that caution, "Harmful if swallowed." Why do we have to be warned about the obvious? Has the United States become a nation of idiots? Do we really need to be told not to fold our children in their strollers?

A few years ago, *NBC Nightly News* did a report on wacky warning labels. Tom Brokaw offered this explanation for why wacky warning labels have become part of our national landscape: "Somewhere in America right now, an untold number of people are on the phone to their lawyers . . . saying, 'Sue 'em.' We are the world's most litigious society, tying up courts, companies, and each other with lawsuits. And it has given rise to a whole new form of literature, the warning label."

That's right. Fear of outrageous lawsuits causes product makers to cringe. And after they're done cringing, these product makers often put labels on the things they manufacture to warn us of the most obvious things. They do this in the hope that if one of their customers does something stupid or clumsy with the company's product, like eating the toner in a printer cartridge, that customer won't sue.

James Percelay, a former writer/producer for *Saturday Night Live* and best-selling author of *Whiplash! America's Most Frivolous Lawsuits*, has explained the reason for these wacky warning labels in a way everyone can understand: "It used to be when someone spilled hot coffee in their lap they called themselves clumsy, today they call themselves a lawyer."

The lawsuits those lawyers file are expensive, even if they never go to a jury trial. Lawyers can file a lawsuit and often settle the case for $10,000, $50,000, and $100,000 or more without ever going before a jury because the company doesn't want to pay the even larger legal bills it would accrue defending itself, even when the company is innocent and the lawsuit has no merit. The following lawsuit against the McDonald's fast-food company illustrates the problem perfectly.

A few years ago, a hungry motorist decided to make a pit stop at a McDonald's drive-thru window. After wedging his chocolate milk shake between his legs and placing his burger and fries on the seat next to him, he resumed his journey. When he leaned over to reach for his fries he inadvertently squeezed his legs together, causing the cold shake to leap out of its cup and onto his lap. Stunned, he then plowed his car into the vehicle in front of him.

The unfortunate motorist who was on the receiving end of this mishap was not sympathetic. He sued the hungry driver as well as McDonald's. The plaintiff's attorney (the lawyer for the guy who was hit) argued that the fast-food franchise neglected to warn customers of the dangers of eating and driving! In making his ruling, the judge did one thing right and one thing wrong. Fortunately, he did dismiss the lawsuit. However, he dropped the ball when he denied McDonald's request to be reimbursed for the $10,000 in attorney's fees to defend itself against this ridiculous lawsuit. In the judge's words, the lawyer who sued the restaurant was, "creative and imaginative and shouldn't be penalized for that."

That, in a nutshell, is why we have so many wacky warning labels. Many lawyers today feel there is no downside to suing someone, because few judges use existing laws that require penalties for those who file frivolous cases. Too many courtrooms have turned into free-for-alls where anyone can attempt to cash in on jackpot justice.

People who make things—whether a lawnmower, a dishwasher, a wheelbarrow, a ladder, or a beverage—know they can be sued by anyone at any time. Even if they win the lawsuit, the companies could spend tens of thousands or even hundreds of thousands of dollars protecting their reputation. Worse, they realize if they get the wrong judge or a bad jury, the person who sued them could hit the "lawsuit lottery" at the product maker's expense. In an effort to protect themselves, these product makers slap all sorts of wacky, outrageous, and often unintentionally hilarious warnings on their merchandise.

Warning! Reading This Book May Cause You to Laugh Hysterically

Despite the obvious humor, your basic sense of what's right and what's wrong may leave you struggling with whether to laugh or cry. It's hard to resist chuckling when you hear that there is actually a warning label on a Christmas tree that reads: "Not intended for human consumption." On the other hand, you may get a little hot under the collar when you read that someone who caught his teeth in a basketball net while dunking later sued the manufacturer and received $50,000 because he wasn't warned that teeth and basketball nets don't go particularly well together. Maybe the warning on the net should have read: "Not intended for use as dental floss."

This book may prompt scores of Americans to consider going to law school so they can become judges who will crack down on the problem of society's frivolous lawsuits. If so, we'll consider this book a public service. Or perhaps it will just provide you with a lot of good laughs. If that's the case, we'll be happy, too.

As Seen on TV . . . These Warnings Are Real

Over the years, wacky warning labels compiled each year by our consumer group, M-LAW, have been featured on news programs on the major television networks in America. The cable news programs love them, too. One of the first questions the shows' producers ask is whether we have seen these labels on actual products. The answer is always yes, but after you read this book, you'll understand why they're skeptical. Some of the labels sound so crazy you might think they are just urban legends.

For the record, M-LAW has verified the authenticity of every label that appears in this book. So when John Stossel was preparing his first story on our wacky warning labels for ABC's popular *20/20* program, we were able to send him every product label he requested. And before Lou Dobbs reported on CNN that a scooter used by youngsters across the United States carries the warning, "Product moves when used," his producer saw it first on our Web site. If we don't see the warning on a product, we don't include it.

This book provides further evidence that truth is indeed stranger than fiction.

Warning Labels You Won't See in This Book

The warning labels in this book represent a small fraction of the labels that have been sent to M-LAW by people nationwide. For our contest, we do not accept warning labels that consumers really need, or that warn against dangers that aren't obvious.

Here's an example of a label we turned down for M-LAW's contest. A bottle of PMS Midol contains a very funny label that warns against using the product if you have an enlarged prostate. You don't need a medical degree to know that if you have a prostate, you aren't going to have premenstrual sydrome, and vice versa. However, there's always the chance some guy out there will get such a bad headache that he'll use anything to get rid of it—even his wife's Midol. Consequently, that warning label needs to be there.

Another label on a tube of toothpaste made specifically for children warns: "Keep away from children." Huh? There are cute little cartoon characters on the casing, and it has the words "Children's Toothpaste" right on the tube. How are my kids going to use this product if I have to keep it away from them? However funny this is, M-LAW didn't include this in our contest because some children, when left alone with a tasty tube of toothpaste, will eat it like candy, and the danger of ingesting too much toothpaste isn't common knowledge.

How M-LAW's Wacky Warning Label Contest Started

Long before the Wacky Warning Label Contest became an annual event, the first winners were selected by the host of a popular program on one of the country's largest radio stations, WJR AM-760 in Detroit. The first year of M-LAW's contest, 1997, was the only year the winners were selected by the radio host, not the audience. For that contest, the top three winners were selected live, on the air, from a list of M-LAW's ten "finalists," by host Mitch Albom and his two co-hosts, Rachel Nevada and Ken Brown. Incidentally, the label Mitch selected was found on a hair dryer and read: "Warning: Do not use while sleeping."

Beginning in 1998, M-LAW added a new twist by letting the radio audience pick the winners of the annual contest. Today, National Radio Hall of Fame personality Dick Purtan lets his huge audience on Oldies 104.3, WOMC, select the wackiest labels from a list of finalists compiled by M-LAW. After M-LAW reads the top five entries, Purtan's listeners call the station to vote for the wackiest label. Money prizes are given to the individuals who send M-LAW the three winning labels.

Each year, the grand-prize winner receives a check for $500 and a copy of the best-selling book *The Death of Common Sense* by Philip K. Howard (though it would probably be more appropriate to award a copy to those who file the kind of frivolous lawsuits that make wacky warning labels necessary).

Philip Howard has also made one of the most astute observations about what wacky labels will reveal to future generations of Americans about our lawsuit-plagued society: "Archaeologists a thousand years from now will dig up our remains and give us a name: Instead of the Age of Reason, we'll be the Age Without Reason. Our amused descendants may not figure out that seesaws disappeared from playgrounds in a fit of legal frenzy, and they may not realize that lawsuits made doctors paranoid and made it difficult for teachers to run a classroom. But what they'll see, in plain language, are the warning labels on every product. They'll really wonder about the coffee. What did we mean by warnings on practically every cup about its being extremely 'hot'? Was coffee some kind of aphrodisiac?"

You can now judge for yourself. What do you think the following 101 wacky warning labels will prompt your descendants to think about life in America during the twentieth and twenty-first centuries?

REMOVE CHILD BEFORE FOLDING

1

Century's TraveLite SPORT baby stroller comes with an owner's manual that has a long section of warnings and instructions on how to fold the stroller.

The first warning:

"Remove child before folding."

Hey, has anyone seen Johnny? He was just here a minute ago!

2

A sun shield made by Solar Stop that can be placed on a car dashboard to keep the sun from turning your car into a sauna on a hot day carries a label that warns:

"Do not drive with sun shield in place."

Coincidentally, right next to this warning is written, in huge letters, a message aimed at attracting the attention of passing motorists should your car become disabled:

"NEED ASSISTANCE."

3

The owner's manual for a hair dryer made by Revlon cautions: **"Never use hair dryer while sleeping."**

Fascinating Fact: This label can be found on virtually all hair dryers, regardless of manufacturer. Most of the warning labels found in this book are unique to the manufacturer that put it there, but not this one.

4

A windproof beach towel tag advises:

"This towel has been tested to withstand significantly strong winds. But please be advised that during a hurricane or other severe weather conditions this product should not be used to secure yourself or anything of value."

The towel may not provide good cover in a hurricane, but will the warning label provide good cover for the manufacturer from a wave of lawsuits?

5

The label on a plastic toy helmet used as a container for popcorn at a professional ice skating show warns:

"Caution: This is not a safety protective device."

The theme of the show was Disney's popular movie *Toy Story*, so the promoters thought it would be cute to sell their popcorn in little military-style helmets for the kids. The lawyers for the manufacturer of the popcorn container obviously wanted to avoid encouraging a sequel called *Lawsuit Story*.

6

A container of Sure underarm deodorant reads:
"Caution: Do not spray in eyes."
Oh, you mean I can't stop my eyes from sweating if I use this?

7

An antifogging cleaner for eyeglasses and ski goggles features a label that reads:

"Caution: NOT for contact lenses or direct use in eye."

So if you get Sure deodorant in your eye, you can't clean it with this product.

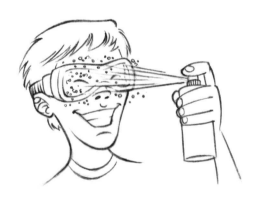

8

The fine print on an Aim n Flame fireplace lighter cautions:
"Do not use near fire, flame, or sparks."
It would be kind of hard to get that toasty fire going on a cold winter's night if you can't use this near fire, don't you think?

9

A Duraflame log carries the warning:

"Caution—Risk of Fire."

Do you think this warning was written by the same person who put the "Do not use around fire or flame" warning on the Aim n Flame lighter?

10

The label on the cartridge for a Ricoh laser printer warns:
"Do not eat toner."
No matter how many times your boss makes you work
through lunch, DO NOT satisfy your hunger by
ripping apart your printer and chowing
down on the toner!

11

A common household iron made by Rowenta Inc. comes with the warning:

"Never iron clothes while they are being worn."

Fascinating Fact: A popular women's fashion magazine contacted me a few years ago to obtain background information about warning labels for a story it was going to publish on the topic. Two weeks after the phone call, a representative called back to say they had canceled the story because the magazine discovered that one of its models had hurt herself when ironing her blouse while wearing it!

12

A Sears Craftsman wheelbarrow that has a thirteen-inch wheel carries this warning on the tire:

"Not intended for highway use."

Imagine the scenario going through the manufacturer's mind when they put this warning on the tire. "Sorry, officer, I blew a tire on my car, and I thought I'd just use the tire from my wheelbarrow to get me the rest of the way to my lawyer's office."

13

The Schwinn bicycle-manufacturing company makes a shin guard with a label that warns:

"Shin pads cannot protect any part of the body they do not cover."

In other words, if you are wearing these pads on your shins and fall and hurt your elbow, don't even think of suing them.

The labels above the public toilets at the WideWorld Sports Center in Ann Arbor, Michigan, warn:

"Recycled flush water, unsafe for drinking."

Ann Arbor is the home to the University of Michigan Wolverines, and we know this warning is going to provide some good punch lines for those Michigan State University Spartans just up the road in East Lansing.

15

The label on a Jet Ski–type personal watercraft reads:
"Warning: Riders of personal watercraft may suffer injury due to forceful injection of water into body cavities either by falling into the water or while mounting the craft."
Ouch! Enough said.

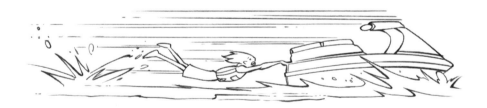

16

A musical birthday candle comes with the warning:
"Do not use soft wax as earplugs or for any other function that involves insertion into a body cavity."
We can probably assume that this wax is not to be used to prevent injuries while riding your personal watercraft, either!

17

A Thomas the Tank birthday badge for a child celebrating his second birthday happily announces on the front that "I am 2." On the reverse it reads:

"Caution: This is not to be used by children under 3 yrs. of age."

At age two, the child wearing this pin probably can't read. That's a good thing considering how little sense this warning makes.

A label on a small handheld massager advises consumers not to use **"while sleeping or unconscious."**

This is one of the cutest products on the market today. The massager is shaped like Garfield the Cat, and "his" battery-operated, three-inch-long feet vibrate to provide a tingly feeling when the product is turned on. However, as for a massage? Be sure to check out the warning label on page 24 for a product that gives a really good massage.

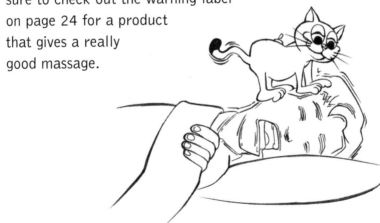

19

The label on a wood router made by Dremel warns:
"This product not intended for use as a dental drill or in medical applications."
Don't have dental insurance? A Texas man didn't, and he thought this little drill would be just the thing to take care of his cavity. It wasn't, and he sued. This definitely falls under the category of "Don't try this at home."

20

A Nikon 35mm camera includes the disclaimer:

"When operating the selector dial with your eye to the viewfinder, care should be taken not to put your finger in your eye accidentally."

This warning was sent to M-LAW by a young boy. He also sent us a photo that showed him carefully using the camera with his heavy-duty safety goggles firmly in place.

21

Nytol's popular Nighttime Sleep-Aid has this obvious warning printed in plain view on the bottle:

"May cause drowsiness."

Let's get this straight. The product is specifically intended to make us so drowsy that we fall asleep. And we're being warned that we might fall asleep?

22

An abdominal breathing exerciser carries this advisory:

"Caution: Do not close your eyes while driving."

All of you multitaskers are hereby warned. Don't sue the makers of this product if you get so relaxed while building six-pack abs and driving at the same time that you want to close your eyes.

23

A Toro snow thrower displays this notice:
"Do not use snow thrower on roof."

Fun Fact: When I do radio interviews around the United States, more people call in to say they've seen a neighbor do this than any other activity in this book.

24

The Interactive Health massage chair comes with this warning: **"Do not use massage chair without clothing,"** and, **"Never force any body part into the backrest area while the rollers are moving."**

This is a wonderful chair that you might have seen at a Sharper Image store. Sit in it, and you just melt.

Apparently, people are finding other creative ways to use this chair.

25

A Bosch dishwasher manual bears this warning:

"Do not allow children to play in the dishwasher."

Aw, come on, Mom, it's raining outside and it looks like so much fun in the dishwasher!

26

The instruction booklet for a Conair brand curling iron for styling hair warns:

"Never use while sleeping."

Even if you want to get a head start on your morning routine, please wake up first!

27

The safety precautions for a common smoke detector made by First Alert warn:

"Do not use the silence feature in emergency situations. It will not extinguish a fire."

You mean if I press the little button on the smoke detector to stop it from making that annoying beeping sound, it won't put out the fire, too??

28

A snow sled for children features a warning that reads:
"Beware: sled may develop high speed under certain snow conditions."
Of course, no child wants his sled to develop high speed, now do they!

29

A twelve-inch rack for storing compact discs carries the warning: **"Do not use as a ladder."**
Outrageous as it may seem, you may need to use that rack as a stepladder one day.

Fascinating Fact: According to U.S. congressman Lamar Smith, the oldest ladder manufacturer in the United States, family-owned John S. Tilley Ladders Company near Albany, New York, recently filed for bankruptcy protection and sold off most of its assets due to litigation costs. Founded in 1855, the Tilley firm could not handle the cost of liability insurance, which had risen from 6 percent of sales a decade ago to 29 percent, while never losing an actual court judgment. The workers of John S. Tilley Ladders never faced a competitor they could not beat in the marketplace, but they were no match for frivolous lawsuits.

30

The warning on a fishing lure with a three-pronged hook on the end reads:

"Harmful if swallowed."

Do you think the fish can read this label?

HARMFUL
IF
SWALLOWED

31

The label on a bottle of drain cleaner warns:
"If you do not understand, or cannot read, all directions, cautions, and warnings, do not use this product."
Obviously, if you can't read the warning, it won't do you much good.

32

The warning on a box of Band-Aid antibiotic bandages reads:
"For external use only."
You'll definitely want to read that warning label before spending
a few hours trying to get a Band-Aid to stick to
the canker sore in your mouth.

33

An instructional video that came with an Alpha Omega car seat for children warns:

"Remove video before use in vehicle."

Fascinating Fact: If you make car seats for a living, maneuvering through America's courts can be a bumpy ride, indeed. According to Steven Hantler, a top attorney at automaker DaimlerChrysler and chairman of the American Justice Partnership, "Volvo makes an integrated child booster seat that is not sold in the U.S. because of product liability concerns." In other words, even if a product is good enough for the rest of the world, it may not be offered to American consumers if the manufacturer refuses to deal with the constant threat of lawsuits.

34

The label on an Adidas tracksuit cautions:

"Please be aware that sliding too fast across indoor floors could cause friction burns where floor, suit, and skin meet."

If you're sliding around in this tracksuit, you might also want to wear special pads like the ones on page 13.

35

The instructions for a popular scooter for children made by Razor warn:

"This product moves when used."

This is the ubiquitous silver scooter used by kids in virtually every neighborhood in America. If you have this product, go ahead and look for the label, which appears on the metal bar between the handles. Just don't try to read it while the product is moving.

36

A label on a small nine-by-three-inch bag of air made by PactivAir3000 and used as packing material carries this warning: **"Do not use this product as a toy, pillow, or flotation device."** This tiny air pouch is smaller than a plastic sandwich bag! It's not exactly the first thing you'd pick for a good night's sleep or even for a life preserver, but if you did, it could be the last thing you'd ever reach for.

The label on the Fantastik Fresh Brush toilet brush reads:
"Do not use for personal hygiene."
It might look like a two-foot-long toothbrush, but really now, do you know where that thing has been lately?

38

The Kitchen Gourmet's electric hand-blender that is promoted for use in "blending, whipping, chopping, and dicing" includes this warning:

"Never remove food or other items from the blades while the product is operating."

If you don't follow this advice, you might find a little more than you bargained for in your casserole.

39

Instructions for the BD digital thermometer, which can measure a person's temperature in at least two different ways, warn: **"Once used rectally, the thermometer should not be used orally."** If you ignore this good piece of advice, whatever you do, please . . . do not try to get rid of that awful taste by reaching for your Fantastik Fresh Brush toilet brush!

40

A bathroom scale carries a label with this warning:

"Caution . . . Care should be exercised when stepping on and off the scale platform to prevent falls."

If you need this warning, you might want to try out the portable Breathalyzer featured on page 99 first.

41

The manual for a professional flat iron made by BaByliss Pro admonishes:

"Never use while sleeping."

That dream you're having about your hair being on fire . . . it's not a dream!

42

A live Christmas tree sold by Nurserymen's Exchange comes with this caveat:

"Not intended for human consumption."

Now, we can see the need for a warning label like this on some Christmas fruitcakes, but on a Christmas *tree*?!

43

The safe handling instructions for a kitchen knife made by J. A. Henckels warn:

"Never try to catch a falling knife."

Pretty obvious, but if you have a friend who "isn't the sharpest knife in the drawer," you might just want to pass along this warning.

44

A cooking pot made by Revere Ware carries this warning:
"Ovenware will get hot when used in oven."
Yes, but will it get cold when put in the freezer?

45

A T-shirt made by Puma displays a tag that cautions:
"Keep away from fire."
We're just guessing, but you might also want to keep away from blowtorches, flamethrowers, and iron smelting ovens.

46

A fan belt manufactured by Kelly Springfield Automotive includes this warning:

"Caution: Before doing any work on belts, be sure the engine is off and cannot be started."

You'll want to change your belts before you get your motor running.

47

An ordinary paper dust mask made by 3M warns:
"Does not supply oxygen."
In other words, if you're going scuba diving, this dust mask won't
replace your oxygen tank.

48

A vacuum sealer made for use in the kitchen by Foodsaver carries this bit of advice:

"Warning: To prevent possible injury, do not apply the hose or lid sealer to any part of the body while vacuum pump is in operation."

It would be easy to make a joke about this warning label, but we wouldn't touch this one with a ten-foot vacuum hose!

49 & 50

A package of rubber fishing worms includes fine print that reads:
"Not for human consumption,"
while a box of Giant Canadian Night Crawlers containing live
bait also cautions:
"Not for human consumption."
Still hungry? That tasty-looking plastic bobber doesn't have
any warnings on it.

51

Many vending machines in the United States display this warning: **"Vending machine will not dispense free product."** This warning is needed because people have been injured while trying to get free sodas by rocking the vending machines and subsequently have sued vendors.

Looney Lawsuit: Being frugal can sometimes cost you more than you bargain for. In 1998, a man was crushed to death after rocking a soda vending machine while apparently attempting to get a free drink. His family filed lawsuits against Coca-Cola and two other companies. The family argued that the companies did nothing to warn people of this danger or prevent it from happening.

52

The print on a shoebox containing slippers made by Hush Puppies warns:

"Do not eat."

It's not clear whether the warning is intended for the box or the slippers. Regardless, it's probably not a good idea to make a meal of either.

53

A box of Dippers frozen mozzarella cheese sticks has a food label that reads:

"Product becomes hot after cooking."

Yes, but can we eat them while we're sleeping?

54

A container of dried bobcat urine that can be sprinkled on the ground to keep animals away from plants and bushes carries the warning:

"Not for human consumption."

But can we eat the yellow snow?

55

The instruction manual for the Nikon Coolpix 5700 digital camera warns:

"Do not place strap around neck: Placing the camera strap around your neck could result in strangulation."

What's next? Warning labels on neckties?

56

The warning label on a bottle of Diet Dr Pepper reads:
"Cap may blow off causing eye or other serious injury. Point away from the face and people, especially while opening."
Is there a Dr. in the house?

57

The tag on a welcome mat made by Team Sports America, Inc., warns:

"The mat should be flat; if you leave it rolled, people can trip."

Fail to follow this advice and you might be welcoming a lawsuit.

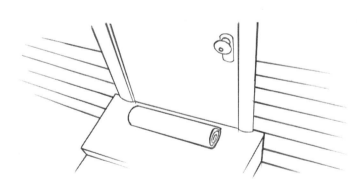

58

A liquid-crystal sensor used to check the temperature of bathwater comes with the warning:

"Always check with your hand before placing child in the tub."

You just shelled out good money for a fancy digital water tester to make sure Junior won't get scalded when he takes his bath. But just to be sure, you're encouraged to use your hand. Think the company is a little concerned about taking a bath in court?

59

The Dino-Chi: T-Rex is a small robotic toy that moves, makes sounds, and even comes with its own plastic food. It also displays this caution:

"Dino-Chi's food is a toy. Dino-Chi's food is not intended for use by a live animal."

Okay. We know some pretty smart dogs. But we've yet to meet one who can read a warning label.

60

A traffic sign in northern Michigan warns:
"Do not pass when opposing traffic is present."
Obvious? Yes. But you can't be too safe when it comes to traffic
signs in Michigan. Need more proof? See below.

Fascinating Fact: Until a few years ago, motorists traveling
Michigan roads used to see signs at bridges warning: "Watch for
ice on bridge." Not anymore. Someone driving over a bridge
spent too much time actually watching for ice, ignored where
they were going, and crashed their car. After the motorist filed a
lawsuit, all the signs near bridges were changed to read:
"Caution. Bridge may be icy."

61

A Polaroid seven-inch portable DVD player comes with this warning:

"Do not swing from the product or pull it."

The DVD player probably shouldn't be used as a projectile in a catapult, either. But for that warning, you'll have to turn to page 93.

62

The warning on a small, battery-operated Shock Stapler
intended for use as a gag reads:
**"Not recommended for children under 6 years / adults over
50 years old . . ."**
Who should feel more offended here?

63

The instruction guide for a BernzOmatic propane torch advises:
"Never use when sleeping."
On the list of things that don't go well together, propane torches and sleeping are probably right at the top.

64

The print on a container of Coralite Tire Shine automotive wipes reads:

"Do not use for personal hygiene."

That is, of course, unless you want to put a shine "where the sun don't shine."

65

The label on the iron-on T-shirt decal found inside a box of Honey Nut Cheerios cereal carries this message:

"Caution: Do not iron while wearing shirt."

If you need more iron, just eat the cereal.

66

All California Super Lotto tickets advise:
"Do not iron."
If your winning ticket gets wrinkled, you might just want to have
it dry-cleaned.

67

A beanbag paperweight made by The Toy Works that looks like a puppy and is called a Pupper-Weight carries this caveat: **"This is not a toy."**

68

The instructions that come with a Cub Scout Pinewood Derby kit admonish:

"Unconventional weight material such as bullet casings and live ammunition are prohibitive."

Wow! If scouts have to be warned not to put bullets in their Pinewood Derby cars, imagine how much their liability insurance policies cost.

Fascinating Fact: The Girl Scouts of Metro Detroit must sell 32,000 boxes of cookies every year just to pay for liability insurance in case they are sued.

69

The tag on a Calvin Klein shirt reads:

"Keep away from fire."

You'll look hot enough in your designer shirt without setting it on fire.

70

This warning sticker was on a new window that was installed on a home in Missouri:

"Warning. Open windows can be hazardous. Failure to heed this warning may result in personal injury or death."

Closed windows can be dangerous, too. See below.

Looney Lawsuit: University of Idaho freshman Jason Wilkins lived in a dorm with windows overlooking the street. Glancing down one afternoon, he noticed a couple of friends passing by. To get their attention he decided to "moon" them and climbed onto a heater, pulled down his pants, leaned his bare butt against the window . . . and fell right through. Wilkins plummeted three floors before landing on the ground, suffering a broken vertebra, compression fractures, deep cuts, and bruises on his hands, legs, and buttocks. Wilkins left college and returned home to recuperate. While on the mend, the former freshman sued the university for not warning residents of the perilous nature of upper-story windows.

71

A package of doggie snacks called Gourmet Bully Sticks has only one ingredient: steer pizzle (that's a polite way of saying steer penis). Don't choke on this warning, but it really reads: **"Not for human consumption."**

72

A can of decorative wall glaze made by Valspar carries these conflicting warnings:

"Avoid drafts from fans, open windows, etc., to prevent premature drying," and, **"Caution: If painting indoors, open windows and doors or use other means to ensure fresh air entry during application and drying."**

Writing warning labels this confusing can take years of practice. Do not, we repeat, do not, try this at home.

73

A small paper cocktail napkin displaying a map of the waterways in the Hilton Head, South Carolina, area carries this note: **"Caution: Not to be used for navigation."** Can't you just see it now: "Hurry, bartender! I'm late for the regatta."

74

The label on a catnip toy made by Vo-Toys reads:
"It is recommended that cats be supervised when playing with all toys."
What good is having nine lives if you can't play with catnip without being supervised?

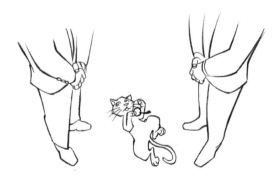

A home barber set made by Conair includes the warning:
"Never use while sleeping."
For those of you who like to keep score, we have been warned so
far to avoid doing the following things while sleeping: drying,
curling, ironing, and cutting our hair, as well as using a handheld
massager or a propane torch. Apparently, it's okay to do
anything else while we're sleeping.

The label on a Marks & Spencer shirt reads:

"In the interest of safety, it is advisable to keep your child away from fire and flames."

Can we assume, therefore, that it's safe to let the kids play around fire if they're not wearing this shirt?!

77

A new graduate of Yale Law School was amused to discover that the mortarboards used at her graduation ceremony came in plastic bags with **an admonition against throwing the four-pointed caps in the air!**

Of course, who would blame a manufacturer for being extra careful with the warnings when dealing with a bunch of new lawyers looking for their first big case!

78

The instruction guide for an electric Microflex men's shaver made by Remington warns:

"Never use while sleeping."

This should just about complete the personal grooming activities we are supposed to avoid while sleeping.

79

The Automobile Club of Southern California provides its members with a wallet-size "guaranteed arrest bond certificate" for use if the motorist is stopped for a minor traffic violation. However, the certificate includes this caveat:

"Not valid in some states, including California."

Considering this, motorists in the Golden State might want to check their insurance policies to make sure they're good in California.

80

A ballpoint pen manufactured by the Quill pen company comes with this advice:

"Warning: Pen caps can obstruct breathing. Keep out of mouth."

Fascinating Fact: The instruction booklet that contains this notice is printed in four languages—French, Spanish, German, and English—but only the English section contains this commonsense warning. From this, we can come to two conclusions: (1) the only people who do clumsy things like swallow their pen caps are English-speaking people, or (2) the only people who do clumsy things like this and then file lawsuits frequently enough to scare manufacturers into slapping wacky warning labels all over their products are English-speaking people. Can you guess which conclusion is correct?

The following label appears on a bottle of Milky Way chocolate milk:

"Contains milk."

Hmmm. Got sense?

82

The label on a screen protector for a personal digital assistant (PDA) reads:

"DO NOT wash protector with PDA! Wash ONLY protector!"

Note to self: DO NOT throw PDA into the washing machine.

A sign posted in the showers at the Georgetown University Conference Hotel in Washington, D.C., reads:

"Please be cautious of the soap dish while in the shower."

Is it a coincidence that this warning was found in a city with more lawyers per capita than in any other city in the United States?

84

The Verizon SuperPages Companion Directory carries this advice: **"Caution: Not for use while operating a moving vehicle."** In other words, don't let your fingers do the walking while you're driving.

85

Popcorn Rock is a naturally occurring mineral found in the Great Basin area of the western United States. A company in Utah sells small chunks of the rock to be used as science projects for children. Pour a little vinegar on the rock, and it grows to look like popcorn. It might look yummy, but the label clearly reads: **"Warning: Eating rocks may lead to broken teeth!"**

86

Many investors who have purchased stock in a U.S. company have seen this warning upon commencing a purchase:

"There is no guarantee past performance will be indicative of future results."

This disclaimer became common during the go-go stock market days of the late 1990s, when many people who planned on getting rich by investing in stock got stung by buying a stinker instead. In a down market, this disclaimer might be viewed more as a sign of hope than as a warning.

87

A hand-cleaning towelette made by Pitney Bowes includes the warning that if it comes into contact with skin,
"Wash hands thoroughly with cold water and soap."
Put another way, if this hand-cleaning towel touches your hands while you are cleaning your hands,
please wash your hands.

88

The notice that comes with baby nail clippers made by Gerber reads:

"Remember: Children are precious and no product replaces adult supervision."

News flash! Children are precious.

89

The label on Dr. Scholl's OneStep Corn Removers carries this warning:

"For external use only."

Finally, a warning label cornier than our jokes!

90

A spa cover made by the company Spa Warehouse displays this label:

"Warning: Avoid drowning. Remove safety cover from spa when in use."

Fascinating Fact: Sunstar, a health-spa manufacturer, decided not to market a safety device due to a liability-related increase in its insurance costs. The product would have set off an alarm every time the cover of a spa was opened. Because the product was a safety device, only one insurance company was willing to write a policy.

The package insert for a Titanium II professional kitchen knife offers this caution:

"Never hold a knife whilst arguing" and **"Never pass a knife to someone blade first."**

Whilst?? The only people we know who talk like that are lawyers.

92

The safety precautions for a heat gun/paint remover that produces temperatures of 1,000 degrees Fahrenheit warn: **"Do not use this tool as a hair dryer."**

Unless, of course, you want a real hair-raising experience.

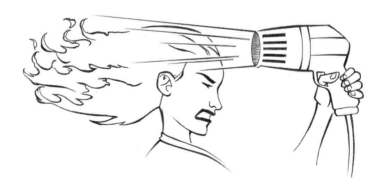

93

The following disclaimer was found on an Ultradisc 2000 CD player:

"Do not use the Ultradisc 2000 as a projectile in a catapult or similar hurling mechanism. Use of the Ultradisc 2000 as a projectile can cause personal injury as well as damage to the transport mechanism, and will void the warranty."

I'm telling you for the last time, Bobby. If you play that rap music again, I'm launching that CD player into orbit.

94

An Evenflo ExerSaucer for toddlers comes with this advice:
"Do not use as a sled."
Oh sure. Go ahead and take all the fun out of slinging our
toddlers down an icy hill.

95

A television commercial for the Hyundai Tiburon automobile displays this warning as the car is shown racing through the streets of a city:

"Professional driver on a closed course. Do not attempt."

This is another one of those warnings you'll find on virtually any car commercial that shows a car (pick one): being driven under water; being driven up the side of a skyscraper; successfully negotiating three consecutive green lights in New York City.

96

The warning label on a washing machine at a Laundromat in Northville, Michigan, reads:

"DO NOT put any person in this washer."

Makes you wonder if the old adage about being "taken to the cleaners" was inspired by a lawyer representing a client who sued after deciding to take a spin in the washing machine!

97

An identification card given by the American Heart Association to individuals who complete a CPR program reads:

"Tampering with this card will alter its appearance."

Let's take a moment to analyze this. If the guy holding a CPR identification card is so dense he needs to be warned that the appearance of the card will change if it is tampered with, do you really want him trying to save your life?!

98

The warning label on a can of self-defense pepper spray reads: **"May irritate eyes."**
The lawsuit that led to the need for this precaution must have been a real tearjerker.

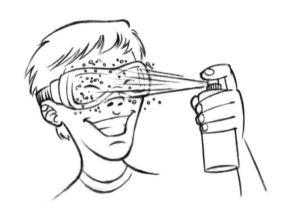

99

A portable digital alcohol detector available at Brookstone stores includes this warning:

"Do not rely upon results to determine intoxication or ability to safely drive a vehicle or operate equipment."

So . . . why did we buy this Breathalyzer in the first place?

100

The warning on a two-by-three-foot inflatable raft reads:
"Not for use in water."
Well, of course not! Why would we want to use a raft in the water?

101

And finally, we end with the warning prompted by Stella Liebeck's world-famous lawsuit against McDonald's over a spilled cup of coffee. Now appearing on coffee cups everywhere: **"Hot beverages are hot!"**

HAVE A FUNNY WARNING LABEL?

Enter M-LAW's annual Wacky Warning Label Contest for your chance to win the grand prize of **$500** and other cash prizes. Visit **www.wackywarnings.com** for more information.

ABOUT THE AUTHOR AND CONTRIBUTOR

Author BOB DORIGO JONES has been studying, writing about, and working to improve America's civil justice system for more than twenty years. After graduating from James Madison College at Michigan State University in 1985, Bob was introduced to the topic of legal reform as a speechwriter for Wayne County executive and Michigan gubernatorial candidate William Lucas. Following that, Bob worked as a writer on the staff of Speaker of the Michigan House of Representatives Paul Hillegonds, and helped document the impact frivolous lawsuits had on the citizens of Michigan. Finally, as president of Michigan Lawsuit Abuse Watch (M-LAW) and as a consultant to several national legal reform groups, Bob has gained worldwide recognition for his campaign to increase public awareness of the high cost that excessive litigation has on our culture.

In 1997, Bob focused media attention on one particular side effect of life in America's lawsuit-happy culture when he launched M-LAW's popular Wacky Warning Label Contest. He is interviewed frequently on television and radio and his work has appeared on virtually every network and cable TV news program in the United States, as well as on many throughout the world. Bob and his wife, Denise, have two children, Robert and John, and reside in a suburb of Detroit, Michigan. Bob enjoys windsurfing, biking, table tennis, and coaching Little League baseball.

Research assistant MICHAEL DALERE is a graduate of Michigan State University who provided invaluable help with the research for this book on his way to law school.